GALLERY OF FORESEE

BY
ZORAN STANIC

Gallery of Foresee by Zoran Stanic

© Copyright 2026, Zoran Stanic, Compiler and Publisher.

This publication is copyright, covering all purposes and conditions prescribed under the Australian law of the Copyright Act 1968 to be only acceptable in usage with permission from the author and publisher Zoran Stanic.

ISBN: paperback   978-1-7644533-9-4
        ebook   978-1-7644533-8-7
        hardcover   978-1-7644533-7-0

Front cover pictures are relating to Chapters 16 & 18.

This revised edition courtesy Immortalise publication assistance service Hackham SA, March 2026

Contents

Introduction v

About Myself vii

Dedication and Thanks xi

Chapter 1 Adam and Eve Presentation –
Prehistoric Time 2

Chapter 2 Atlantians and Atlantis 5

Chapter 3 Space Watchers 8

Chapter 4 Creation of The Environmental Surface – Prehistoric
Time 10

Chapter 5 Sleeping City Twin Towers NY USA 12

Chapter 6 Silky Translucent Entities 14

Chapter 7 Is Our DNA Who We Are? 16

Chapter 8 Time Keylock – Time Code 18

Chapter 9 Haarp Surface Shaper-Creator –
Prehistoric Time 22

Chapter 10 The Ocean Under The Ocean –
Prehistoric Time 24

Chapter 11 Magic Creation..................26

Chapter 12 Parallel Universe..................28

Chapter 13 Unsuccessful Project..................30

Chapter 14 Mars Project..................32

Chapter 15 Super Advanced Sun Expedition..................34

Chapter 16 Human Star Gates..................36

Chapter 17 Compromise Between True Heaven and Hell..................38

Important Message..................76

Chapter 19 Under Sea Star Gates and Bases..................44

Chapter 20 Stars Wars Superiority..................46

Chapter 21 Fauna and Flora of The First Settlements – Prehistoric Time..................48

Chapter 22 Antarctica Civilizations..................50

Chapter 23 Olmecs Arrival By Plasma Star Gate..................52

Chapter 24 Endless Reciprocals..................54

The Proofs of My Original Pictures..................59

Comparison of Civilisations, Humanoid Species and Entities..................61

My Thoughts On Mixed Topics..................71

Introduction

All of my vivid predictions from almost 47 years ago have come true in the last 7 years. I'm still trying to figure out this mysterious phenomenon, and understand why these events have been happening over the past 5-7 years.

They have often left me confused and in denial. It makes me think, how could so many of my predictions and original ideas suddenly become reality? Have we reached a turning point of similar ideas and thoughts?

I would like to point out that the energy of my predictions came to me out of the blue, moved me, and shook me into this lifelong project without any knowledge and preparation. Without any sign or notice, information, science, news, booklets, computers, TV and radio stations; somehow, all of these disadvantages did not stop the cosmic energy from passing to me the predictions and thoughts that I have exposed in this book.

There could have been some involvement with my subconscious, or something genetically inherited, such as energy passed down by ancestors, like a special gift to be used one day to make my dream book come alive.

About Myself

Zoran Stanic was born and raised in Europe.

In 1988, he settled in Sydney, Australia.

He studied in both Europe and Australia, qualifying in the professions of Mechanical Engineering, Interpreting and Translating, English Teaching, and Security Management.

Zoran's hobbies include writing, various arts, music, traveling, history and Science.

He sees people as either good or bad, and has no time for emptiness. He doesn't believe in politics and artificial money.

He believes in God and Mother Nature.

He believes in PEACE and the formation of a CIVILISED WORLD without wars, human suffering, and poverty.

Dedication and Thanks

I would like to dedicate this book to:

My parents, as they left this world of the living a couple of decades ago, and to my first son who died too young, following his grandparents shadows, somewhere in the place I call: Stanic's Silky Translucent Section of Shades in God's Astral Kingdom.

To be always remembered with no disappearance from my thoughts and my soul.

I would like to thank my best friends.

Zoran Jekovic, for supplying me with the key evidence that makes my book Predictive, Original, Unique, and Authentic.

Daniel Rendell, who involved me in his own book projects as an illustrator, and encouraged me to share my story "WHEN STARS COLLIDE".

Chapter 1
Adam and Eve Presentation – Prehistoric Time

(Author's Original Artwork – 1978)

By NASA/Ames/JPL-Caltech – http://kepler.nasa.gov/news/nasakeplernews/index. cfm?FuseAction=ShowNews&NewsID=165, Public Domain, https://commons.wikimedia.org/w/index.php?curid=24187911 "PUBLIC DOMAIN"

In the Kepler solar system, the planets KEPLER 22B, KEPLER 186F, and in the NIBIRUM solar system, Rocky Planet, and DAYSTAR – the "water world" planet are potential celestial bodies from which visitors from outer-space came to earth long ago.

The ANUNNAKI came from the Nibirum Solar System in transit to us earth people.

The Kepler Solar System is further up, in a vertical orbit above us.

ADAM/S and EVE/S could've come from those above solar systems. The ANUNNAKI, along with the young ones who came to our planet almost 500,000 years ago with the older ones, were given the privilege of getting married in a place called the GARDEN of EDEN, which today is actually Bahrain Island, a small country in the Persian Gulf.

The Garden of Eden was an EXPERIMENTAL LABORATORY ISLAND to Experiment and work on different races, skin colour, DNA, Flora and Fauna, and new patterns of all kinds of innovations and demonstrations.

There were, and are many research labs called the "UNDERGROUND EDEN" & "MOON BASEMENT". There are also GARDENS of EDEN in Kepler 22b and 186f planets, the Daystar planet UNDERWATER SCOOBA EDEN, and the Nibirum COMPLETED PROJECT of Garden of Eden.

The Earth Planet Garden of Eden started at a place called the Island State of Bahrain in the Persian Gulf. Also, taking place in the Arabian Peninsula, Mesopotamia – the land of the Assyrians, the land of Canaan, the land of the Kemets, ect.

Jesus' bloodline could be related to his ancestors from the Garden of Eden. The Turin Shroud of Jesus was a three

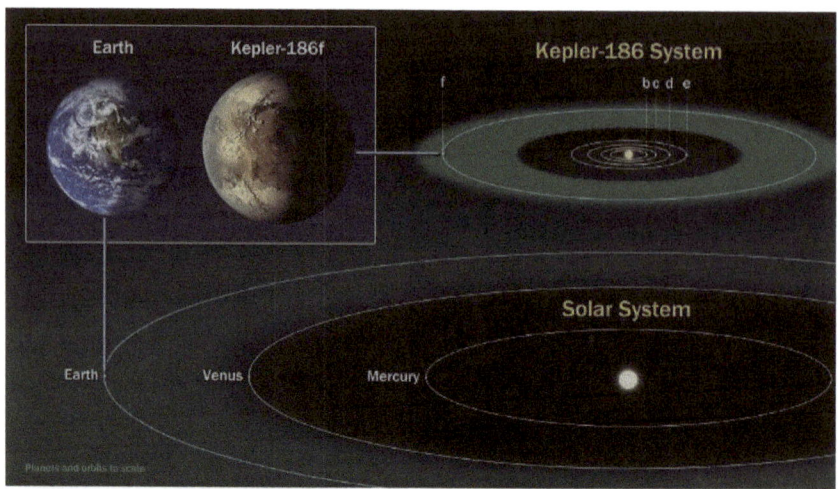

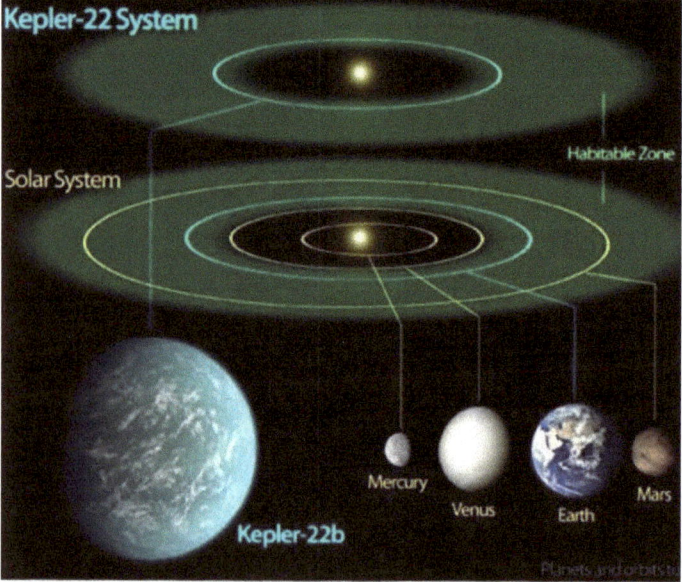

By NASA/Ames/JPL-Caltech –
http://kepler.nasa.gov/news/nasakeplernews/index.cfm?
FuseAction=ShowNews&NewsID=165, Public Domain, https://commons.
wikimedia.org/w/index.php?curid=24187911 "PUBLIC DOMAIN"

dimensional Leonardo da Vinci GEOMETRICAL CODE EXPERIMENT, which was typical for his ADVANCED EXPERIMENTS and CREATIVITIES. It is comparable with a well known Da Vinci PROPORTIONAL MALE/FEMALE CODE.

Chapter 2
Atlantians and Atlantis

(Author's Original Artwork – 1978)

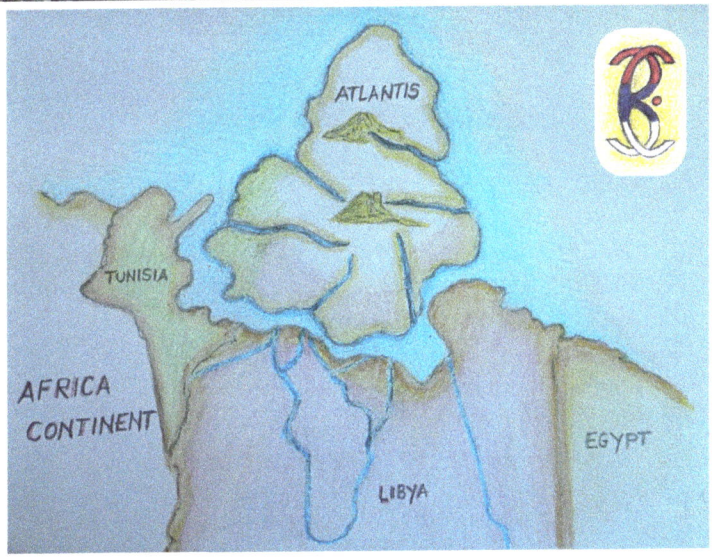

Nibirum Solar System

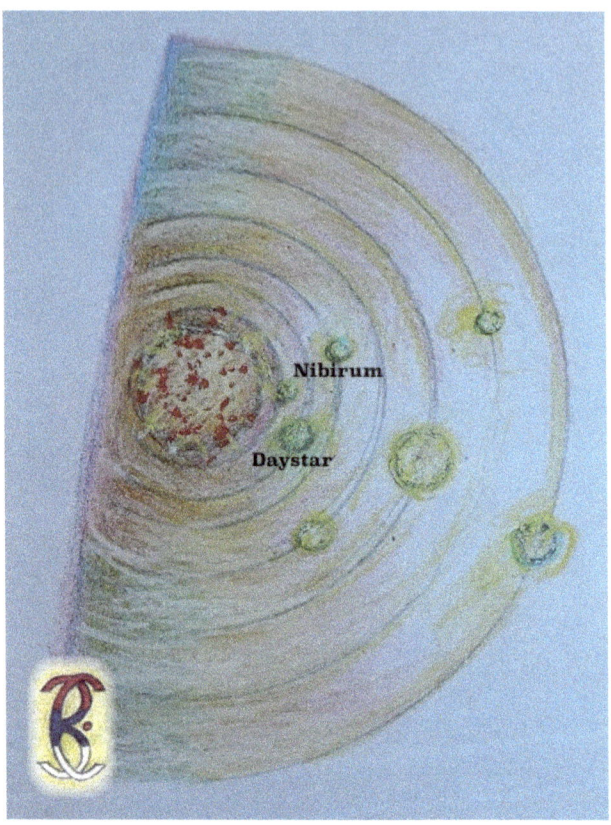

The Atlantians were based in the Mediterranean Sea of the surrounded borders area on the South Libya, up on North Sicily-Italy, left on West Malta and right on East Greece. That's why they couldn't have travelled by big boats or sailing ships at that time.

The Canary Islands were something else. At that time is was an unknown place with unknown settlements. It could be another race from space. In those days the Gibraltar passage was closed and it was impossible to cross by boat or even with ships at that time.

War broke out between the new settlement, called the Atlantians, and the Mediterranean coloniser, which was colonised by PRE ANUNNAKIS or the PRE KRISHNA civilisation.

In that war, the Mediterraneans destroyed Atlantis and their main island. Before the Atlantians left with their mother ship, they undermined the Gibraltar barriers using a powerful weapon, which caused a big flood that reached Dardanelles Mountain Range.

Barriers at Dardanelles Passage did not exist in that time and with the other massive explosion breaking up Dardanelles mountain range, the valley settlements filled up with a massive amount of Mediterranean sea water, as that area became a new sea called the Black Sea, and a new passage belongs to that sea today, called the Dardanelles Passage.

After the Atlantians' mothership took off with their settlements somewhere next to our solar system, perhaps they went back to the NIBIRUM solar system to the water world planet they belong too.

In 2025, I found that WATER WORLD PLANET in NIBIRUM SOLAR SYSTEM exists. It's called "DAYSTAR". The Atlantians had a Leader, King, Father, and God, called ATLAN, which means "A KING of WATER".

Chapter 3
Space Watchers

(Author's Original Artwork – 1978)

With thoughts of wonder we look up into the deep, vast expanse of endless space at night. Since our creation we have looked to the heavens for answers. Deep within our ancestry we know that we came from the stars, that we were created in an experimental laboratory or an EVOLUTIONARY LAB.

That E.LAB was operating until they formed our perfect, physical and intellectual human bodies or PRODUCT. Labs were normally based on earth as the secret temples, underground stations, and cities.

Some labs were/are in the moon, underground cities, and experimental departments. Also, KEPLER'S planetary solar system with its various planets is still in existence today, as it was then.

KEPLER 22b, KEPLER 186f and so on were capable of supporting and sustaining EXPERIMENTAL LABS and underground cities to fulfill their projects.

There is no space extension in a divided, vast universe, because of the galactic cannibalism of black holes, moderating all births and deaths of galaxies and planets, as well as the vast universal boundaries.

Out there are sub-universes – frozen Sections to be awakened by gravitational forces passed from the ACTIVE MULTI-GRAVITY NEIGHBOURHOOD OF GALAXIES.

Chapter 4
Creation Of The Environmental Surface- Prehistoric Time

(Author's Original Artwork – 1978)

THE LANDSCAPE SOIL has been sustained and stabilised with a fertilising and planting mixture of protein feed, which sparks the growth of plants as future forests, orchards, fields, and natural agriculture.

Who planted that special mixture of protein feed? It had to have been planted by pre-planned and advanced structural projects in a prehistoric time.

The programme of that perfect supply has been used for millions of years. The goodness of that protein mixture was a substantial gift for life to exist on our planet.

It became a major food supplier for living creatures and their future generations in an ENDLESS CIRCLE OF A GIFTED EXISTENCE.

In certain times, from now to ten decades in the future, food will be limited, which will, in turn, limit our global population. The elite will be cutting off food and populations through different options relating to the pharmaceutical industry. Tablets, capsules, liquids, powders, etc, instead of natural food ingredients.

After that, we will be slowly replaced by intelligent robots, which need no food, water, or air to survive. The plan is to eliminate all natural life and replace it with a futuristic, artificial workforce.

Socratea exorrhiza is a palm tree that can walk up to twenty metres per year, which is a couple of centimetres per day. They can reach heights over twenty-five metres and can live between one-hundred and six-hundred years. Trees make their own food through photosynthesis, using energy from the sun, water (from roots), and carbon dioxide (from the air) to create sugar that's used to fuel the entire tree.

Chapter 5
Sleeping City – Twin Towers NY USA

(Author's Original Artwork — 1979)

New York's most important landmark was basically the biggest, richest, and most active gambling trade casino in the world; a place where trillions of dollars were gambled away like nothing.

The twin towers were a "MONEY BAIT" for those who planned to bring down the casino and collect a staggering amount of money. It was a well-organised inside job.

My guts feelings at that time were telling me that huge amounts of money were circulating through the biggest landmark trade casino and that it wouldn't last much longer.

How can a HIGH FLYER with a single finger pressing a button become an instant millionaire or billionaire?

I thought: one day it will burn up with a big fire on many levels, as revenge for those who lost a lot of money. My picture shows smoke points starting from the top levels of the buildings.

There is also a strange man holding a lion on a leash, subconsciously telling me that somebody is going to cross that line – and sabotage something – POWERFUL PEOPLE WILL DO THAT.

Just as the UFO shows the Aliens involvement, and people of different nations and backgrounds, where there is too much money – there is a devil, and where the devil is – there is always a FIRE.

Why did they choose the date of 9/11?

911 – Is an EMERGENCY CALL and a VERY IMPORTANT number.

Why did they choose the year 2001?

2001 – Is a very IMPORTANT YEAR OF BEGINNING. It marks the 21st CENTURY, and the 21st century will always be remembered for the events that took place on that fateful day.

Most of the irresponsibility in the world is shared between **"Demons influence possessed people by money, not knowing it, and touch of politics!"**

Free to use under Unsplash Licence
www.unspash.com

13

Chapter 6
Silky Translucent Entities

(Author's Original Artwork – 1979)

SILKY TRANSLUCENT BODIES APPEARANCE. THEY CAN TRAVEL INTO MANY DIMENSIONS, INCLUDING HUMAN DREAMS.

The micro neutron structure of energy can be converted into all kinds of SILKY LIGHTNING BODIES. It's not achievable for us with our low IQ levels.

The systematic and code advanced way to shift and restore from micro protons, neutrons, and Electrons, almost equals a micro atom to visibly shed cornopeal form as a static or dynamic structure.

(1994 – Experienced on the Singaporean airline heading from Australia to Europe)

15 year later, (1994) away from my thoughts, I had myself experienced and stepped into that CRYSTAL GLITTERY ZONE OF THE TRANSLUCENT WORLD DIMENSION with sea shell sounds and static, filled with translucent entities. It was a short blink of light time-trip, which I call "A CLINICAL CRYSTAL TRIP."

Chapter 7
Is Our DNA Who We Are?

(Author's Original Artwork – 1979)

"GENERALLY SPEAKING, THE BEGINNING OF CREATION STARTS WITH A NEST AND AN EGG UNTIL IT REACHES A HUMAN-FORM STAGE!"

If we look at the very remote tribes in jungles around the world, like the Amazon, South America, Borneo, Papua New Guinea, Asia, the African Congo, etc, the appearances of those tribes and their natural look hasn't changed for thousands of years.

They could be unformed in many types of physical or intellectual ways. If we compare them to modern humanoids, they would be behind modern human form and not be relatable, unwilling to have any kind of interaction with Star Entities or to experience intercourse with them. HUMAN HYBRIDS are a mix of those two races. But it would not work out if the human form had not been perfected.

Thanks to resources from the Ancient past we have gained some knowledge from the Sumerian tablets, including the Bible, and many are familiar with THE SUICIDE MISSION OF THE FALLEN ANGELS – THE MASSIVE AMOUNT OF BLOOD FROM GIANTS' BODIES WERE COVERING the landing zones around certain parts of the world in that time. I call it "THE HELL OF THE PLANNED EXPERIMENTS".
STAR ENTITIES also brought their females to fulfill the population experiments, just the other way around.

The question is: "Why were the WATCHERS observing the entire calamity?"

Maybe it was a kind of PUNISHMENT or fruitless experiment?

In the end, they raped THE EARTH of Indigenous females, and got them impregnated with giant, mortal newborn babies.

How could such an interaction between two different entities take place when most of the FALLEN ANGELS DIED IN THAT SUICIDE MISSION? Only if they fell into deep water, not shallow water, or crashed against the rocks of the shore, would they be able to achieve their objective.

DNA was different in both cases. The STAR ENTITIES CHANGED THE EARTH'S INDIGENOUS DNA for the next experiments and further interaction. There were no findings of any DNA PROOFS or ARTIFACTS to convince us that DNA in the Earth's population, especially the female population, had been interrupted.

People and civilisations of earth were, and are, the experiments of high intelligent entities, leading us "from dust to dust, and ashes to ashes."

The meaning is: "we will be used until we all disappear, which means the project's done!"

The question is: do we exist at all, or are we traveling as a human's energy net fabric?

Chapter 8
Time Keylock – Time Code

(Author's Original Artwork – 1979)

Mother Earth's KEY-LOCK SHAPE-PUZZLE CODES:

We, as EARTH CITIZENS, have been struck with many kinds of past abuses.

When we reach a certain point or get close to the answer, we have been distracted with something that directs our attention away from the KEY ANSWER to opening that MYSTERY LOCK.

Sadly, it always remains in the air untouched, and unsolved. These FIVE MAIN FORMS are presented on my picture.

1. Since 500,000 years ago, the Earth has experienced constant visitations from space. It has been a routine plan from A GLOBAL SPACE AGENDA OF INTERFERENCE BY STAR ENTITIES.

   They came from outer-space. Their mission has been to stay here and build their landmark bases, as our planet became their long-term "RESEARCH LAND LAB PROJECT."

   Kepler 186f was the original base of THE STAR ENTITIES, who came to our planet. The top details of the circle key lock picture shows similarities in landscapes to Kepler 186f.

2. BOOMERANG is a symbol of SPACE ENTITIES CONTACT with Australia's Aboriginals, proving that one of their visitations took place around 45000 years ago when they gave the aborigines that MAGIC FLYING TOOL called the BOOMERANG.

   The boomerang could be the shape of A MOTHER SPACE SHIP that came from KEPLER 186f.

   With a meaning: "WE WILL ALWAYS MAGICALLY COME BACK TO YOU!" A MAGIC DIDGERIDOO was the Aboriginals' "sound present" of WELCOMING to the SPACE ENTITIES.

3. ATLANTIS Island was an ANCIENT STATE formed 22000 years ago; one of the first civilised states, and civilisations on Earth. Two advanced groups of space entities fought each other, causing the destructions of Atlantis, before a MOTHER SPACESHIP collected the ATLANTIANS and took them to their home Water-World Planet, or somewhere else to continue their routine project of spreading knowledge to other advanced civilisations.

4. The PYRAMIDS are ENERGY SUPPLIERS AND RECEPTERS around the world. They were all built around the same time, excluding the abandoned pioneer ones, which are now covered with soil and trees. Today they are hardly recognised, but some have been discovered in Bosnia, Herzegovina, China, Indonesia, etc. They could be over 20000 years older than existing ones, as we can see them today around the world in Egypt, Mexico, South America, Asia, etc.

5. MEGALITHS around the world had a role to play in promoting powerful and advanced tools, which were used to carve giant stones for their creation. The giant stones were placed using advanced lifting technology, so that humans would never be able to remove or transport them to another place.

Such landmarks have been left on purpose by star entities to show how intellectually disadvantaged humans are.

All of those above, pointing out the mysteries are one of the major "CODEX SECRETS". If we could work to solve that High Advanced Enigma, it would lead us to the opening of a horizon of unsolved codex mysteries, which could be shared with all humanity.

Chapter 9
(HAARP) Surface Shaper Creator – Prehistoric Time

(Author's Original Artwork – 1979)

At that time I didn't know what to call it. To me, it was a special robotic device which forms landscapes on our planet, and activates volcanoes.

The first time such a device was used was half a million years ago. The purpose was to create the earth's landscape, and natural resources around the globe. The device was equipped with powerful magnetic plasma, and laser forces.

To be able to create shapes out of the mountains, rivers, canyons, lakes, etc, would be supplied by fresh or salty water through the created weather pattern, including the seasons relating to the environment and leveled places.

Those places we now call continents, islands, North and South Poles. Everything has been perfectly designed and projected by high intelligent technology that never reached our consciousness to be used in our present, but possibly in our future.

Lakes, rivers, seas, and oceans have been experimentally designed and integrated with elements we can find today in both salt and fresh waters, and also in sulphur/acid waters, which are the original liquids left over. Those waters are resistant against environmental disadvantages, but favourable for our usage.

In our future, we will be able to reshape mountains, canyons, fields, rocky and sandy deserts. We will be able to make it rain in specific areas and alter the environment without the use of explosives, machinery, robots, or human physical force. One device will do everything for us.

Chapter 10
The Ocean Under The Ocean

(Author's Original Artwork – 1979)

BENEATH THE KNOWN-PRESENT OCEANS, UNDER THE OCEANS CRUSTS THERE IS A SECOND LEVEL OF OCEAN.

That second layer of ocean has 3 times more water than the original ocean above. It could be from a different origin, and the water is likely to be much warmer.

The living creatures there are different in shape, colour, and age. I call it the "ANCIENT OCEAN" before all the new seas. As you look at my picture there is a shape of God between the oceans and a CHILD SHAPE – PRESENTING THE

NEW OCEAN seated next to the shape of victory fingers, telling us there are TWO OCEANS, one under the other.

According to my thoughts, the second ocean beneath the other is like ARCHAEOLOGICAL LAYERS as a SEA-BED RESERVOIR made from soil and rocks, but in the case of my picture it's THE EARTH'S CRUST – THE FORMATION OF ROCKS AND THE OTHER SEDIMENTS DIVIDING TWO DIFFERENT LIQUIDS OR RESERVOIR POOLS.

The first experimentally made ocean was the original one. Our present ocean was created afterwards, as the perfect lab experimental product, including all sequences to be ENVIRONMENTALLY USED.

In the picture you will notice a middle finger and a pointing finger, indicating an attention to that important picture detail.

There are authentic divides between the surface of the ocean and ocean under the sea, which was made directly by a God interference, who we call our CREATOR.

There are many archaeological graves under the sea, lakes, and rivers.

The second ocean was finally discovered in 2014.

Free to use under Unsplash Licence www.unspash.com

Chapter 11
Magic Creation

(Author's Original Artwork – 1979)

Pyramids were built on a natural hill by ancient African people similar to the Dogon tribe. They live today, as do the West African and other tribes.

The Nubians also lived in North East Africa. In the past, they were exchanging high advanced knowledge and learned a lot from Space Entities.

They used their knowledge and masonry skills to build the Giza Pyramids with constant cooperation and the observation of advanced space entities. In that time, tribes were using secret knowledge and kept it hidden until these very last days.

The Egyptians did not build the Giza Pyramids; they found them after THE BIG FLOOD.

The Advanced Entities Technology has been gained by some African tribes, including the Dogons, Nubians, Badari, Naquada, who all gained that special knowledge thousands of years ago.

The space entities are still here, moving in and out of their different dimensions inaccessible to us, but when using our dimension they will sometimes be seen.

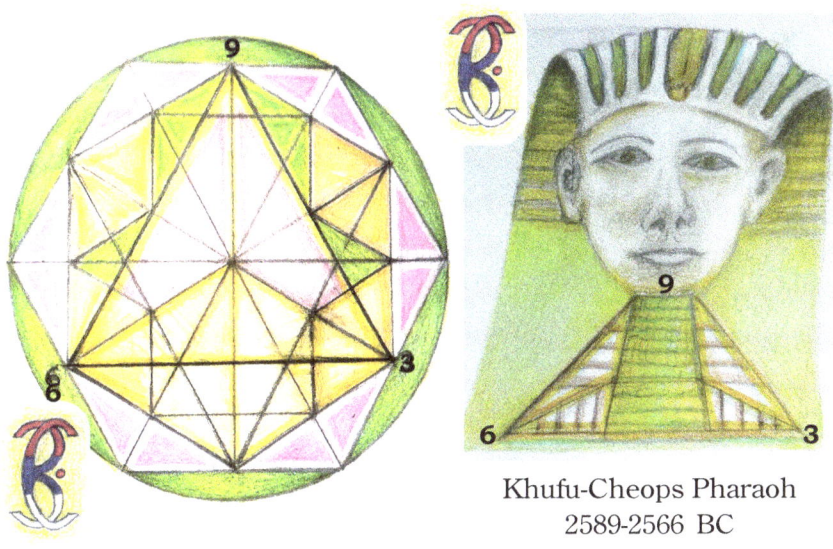

Khufu-Cheops Pharaoh
2589-2566 BC

"TIME-POWER-CONTROL-EXISTENCE"

Chapter 12
Parallel Universe

(Author's Original Artwork – 1979)

RABBIT PARALLEL UNIVERSE

A parallel universe is what my picture shows. It presents a mirror of turnaround or upside down parallel universe with only one shape into two different expressions.

It's means that it symmetrically exists like that, but is meaningfully, and shapely divided.

CRAB PARALLEL UNIVERSE

They can be parallel but not the same. Because of the position, it must be rotated to distinguish the structural shape. We can see that one rotation is a rabbit, and the other is a crab.

Chapter 13
Unsuccessful Project

(Author's Original Artwork – 1979)

A planetary system is a very complex form with many challenges. Sometimes the project does not go smoothly, even with an advanced technology plan.

Unpredicted attacks from higher advanced civilisations, such as star wars can halt projects, or have projects taken over by a new, more advanced conqueror.

Temporary star wars or perpetual star wars may continue to exist until the extinction of the warring species, causing the abrupt end or annihilation of a project. The consequences of radioactive involvement can lead to the poisoning of lands and waters, rendering any project useless. Such circumstances can lead to a planetary death, which can last for centuries.

Some projects simply do not go according to plan, in which case the space entities may opt to reset the project via annihilation through natural disasters.

In the past, and today, we have been heavily manipulated and experimented on by the same space entities. They built civilisations, and then destroyed them through wars or on purpose to fulfill the upgrading of a repeating project.

We can only estimate as to how many civilisations have been destroyed over and over.

We can only speculate and approximate according to some historical and chronological proofs that survived from ancient times. Most have all disappeared without a trace physically, but not architecturally.

THE PROOFS OF THE UNSUCCESSFUL PROJECTS IN OUR PERHISTORIC TIME HERE ON THE EARTH WERE PETROFIDED GAINTS, ANIMALS, TREES ECT.

Chapter 14
Mars Project

(Author's Original Artwork – 1979)

Harsh, unpredictable planets like Mars, which have terrible weather conditions, radiation, no drinking liquid, food, and no oxygen, should not be colonised by people, at least until the atmosphere and planet has become tolerable for human habitation.

Before humans step foot on such planets as Mars, further research needs to be conducted by a coalition/organised space programme involving the very brightest minds from around the globe. Different types of specialist robots should be the first to inhabit Mars, as opposed to human astronauts.

To accomplish the goal of Mars colonisation, robots should be first, followed by genetically altered birds and other animals that do not require oxygen to breath. With the help of artificial intelligence, robots should always be the first choice, as they do not require oxygen or food.

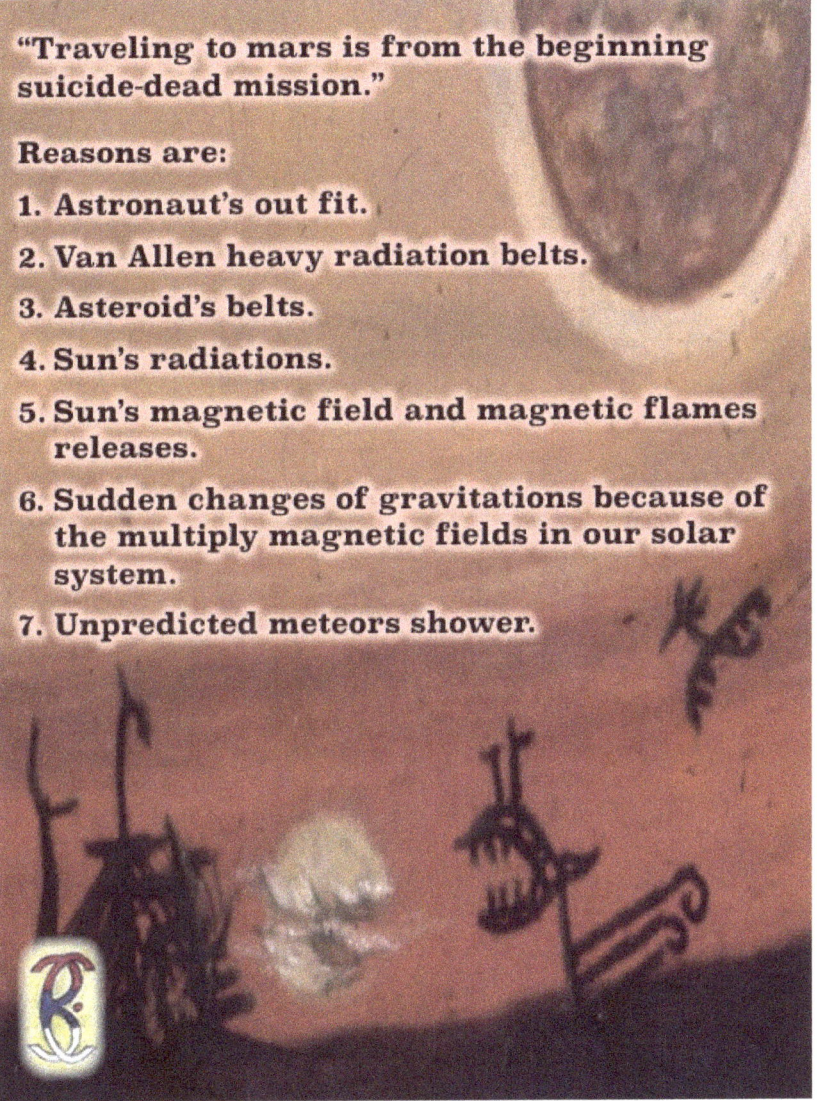

"Traveling to mars is from the beginning suicide-dead mission."

Reasons are:

1. Astronaut's out fit.
2. Van Allen heavy radiation belts.
3. Asteroid's belts.
4. Sun's radiations.
5. Sun's magnetic field and magnetic flames releases.
6. Sudden changes of gravitations because of the multiply magnetic fields in our solar system.
7. Unpredicted meteors shower.

Chapter 15
Super Advanced Sun Expedition

(Author's Original Artwork – 1979)

A massive interplanetary mothership landed on our sun on the cooler, darker side of the sun's surface to refill its radioactive fuel.

It's a part of the experiment diagnosing our sun's temperature changes, radiation levels, magnetic field changes, and taking samples. Important radioactive fuel supplements allow them to continue their planetary and interplanetary space trips.

Research and observations of the galaxies and planets, and their important landmarks are always ongoing. They are regularly observing different projects throughout the universe, including their projects on earth. Every Galactic sun is a mega fuel station supplier.

Photo: Super high technology spacecraft 2012, taking samples and refilling fuel from the Sun's surface:

The Sun burns Hydrogen, which is a perfect fuel for a starship. The Sun's temperature is 3 million degrees.

Solar magnetic bubble full of super hot magnetic plasma.

"WAS IT UFO PHENOMENA OR SOLAR MAGNETIC BUBBLE!?"

Chapter 16
Human Star Gates

(Author's Original Artwork – 1979)

In the urban pre-ancient and ancient cities, to this day, we have the construction of gates that represent human "Stargates" were built as a template to pass on to us thousands of years in the past. If we look at the entrances of cities, temples, and the private properties of the elite, we can see that they were built in honour of those who came here from outer space and gave us symbolic visual memories of knowledge to build what we thought were simply decorative.

MAGNETIC AND PLASMA FUTURISTIC STARGATE:

Stargates will come back in a multi-dimensional and unseen form. The energy that's part of those gates is the decoration of the material combined with a spiritual energy concentrated in the forms of energies related to telekinesis, telepathy, levitation, cosmic energy, as well as magnetic and plasmatic energy of the highly superior technologies and their intelligent users and owners.

Are they semi-hybrid cosmic beings or highly intelligent robots or some kind of beings unknown to us, never or rarely seen by human eyes, because of their ability to disappear using other unknown dimensions that we have never experienced?

"Stargate entities will be back before the angels are going to die. Who is the angel or angels? The celestial beings of light found in many religions?"

Chapter 17
Compromise Between True Heaven and Hell

(Author's Original Artwork – 1979)

What is really A HELL and what is really A HEAVEN as a DEFINITION?

It's so difficult to arrange the meaning up to the place of usage and the meaning for it. Sometimes those vocabularies can exchange positions of their meaning status. There were, and still are underground tunnels and towns. Today, we terminologically exchanged that into graveyards/burials.

Why did humans build underground shelters? In Turkey there still exists an underground town with long corridors able to accommodate thousands of people, and protect them from a fast spreadable disease, like black plague. It also protects them from debris falling from space.

In the distant past, we learned that hell is under our feet and that heaven is above our heads, up in the sky. But in the 20th century those terms are being pulled in the opposite directions. The term Hell was relatively pointed out to bankers of atomic shelters, which act as a SAFE HAVEN OR "HEAVEN".

Controversially, the heaven has never been placed in underground; the underground was always Hell. Most threats in the past were coming from the sky. Meteors, comets, heavy winds, space junk, natural lightning, falling Angels, and falling spaceships, etc.

Hazards eventually caused the names of heaven and hell, along with their destinations, to be exchanged. The technology of the ancient past and the technology of today are nuclear technologies that can cause vast destruction.

Warfare and atomic shelters go hand in hand. In the Stone Age, cave people were hiding inside caves most of the time using natural shelters as resources -NOT KNOWING that the caves had been created just for them. At that time, people were not buried underground, but their bodies were kept in a different section of the same cave for ritual reasons.

How were caves created for them? It was simply part of the creator's project. People were buried underground to remain there for thousands of years as a long-term Conservation.

WHAT HAPPENS TO A HUMAN SPIRIT?

The human spirit gets connected to the cosmic energy traveling through the energy dimension chambers to reach the FED CORNOPEAL TRANSLUCENT DIMENSION, where it will finally be formed as an active project, and will be able to move or travel around, and be seen in different forms, like a passive state. In some cases, they are filled with a temporary active energy, and then they slowly become animated, and at the same time be again REFORMED and ACTIVATED by AN ADVANCE "SILK NET CROSSING TRANSLUCENT ENERGY."

The underound site known as Elengubu. It's an ancient multi-

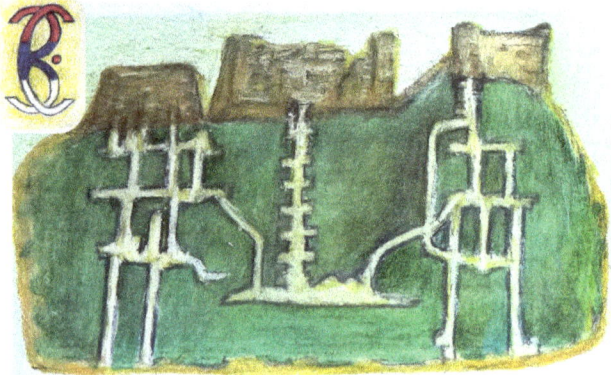

level underground city over 3000 years old found in Turkey. The depth of that underground site is approximately 85 metres and can fit between 20,000-30,000 people.

Chapter 18
Sharing DNA

(Author's Original Artwork – 1979)

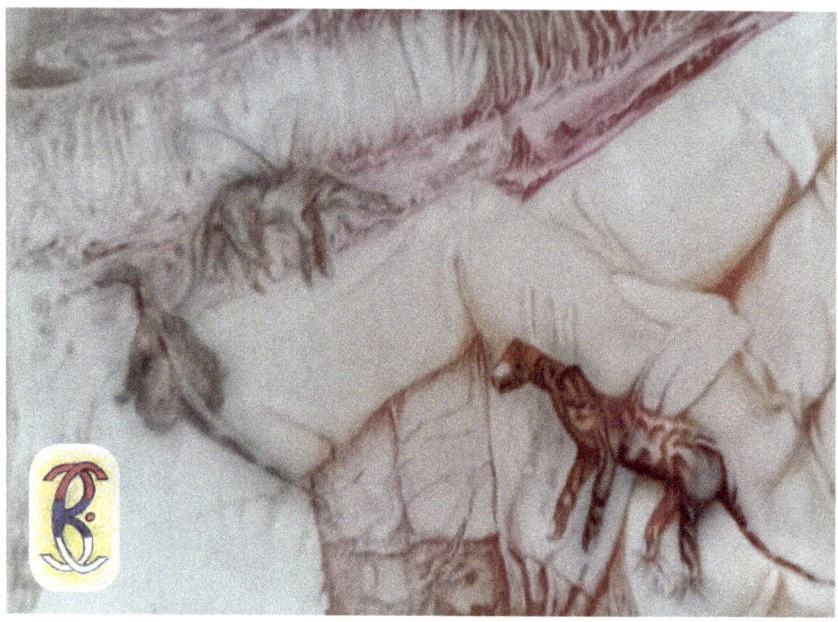

Did we really share or are we still sharing our DNA with a cosmic microchip!? Everything surrounding us is part of the environment of our existence with highly provided supplements in flora and fauna, sharing DNA codes and markers between us.

We are all part of big DNA FAMILIES that have been made up to exist and live together in harmony, all relying and relating on DNA segments. Our abilities allow us to use many kinds of options and ways to cooperate with our basic daily life using natural food recourses.

Multiple DNA influences to non-humans will continue until it reaches A MAXIMUM PERCENTAGE OF EQUALITIES to transform fauna and flora into themselves, ENTITIES with ABILITIES OF HUMAN SPEECH AND MOVEMENTS.

The shape of DNA is called a double helix. It resembles a twisted ladder or spiral staircase carrying information from the past to the present, and into the future. It has been modified and can be modified again.

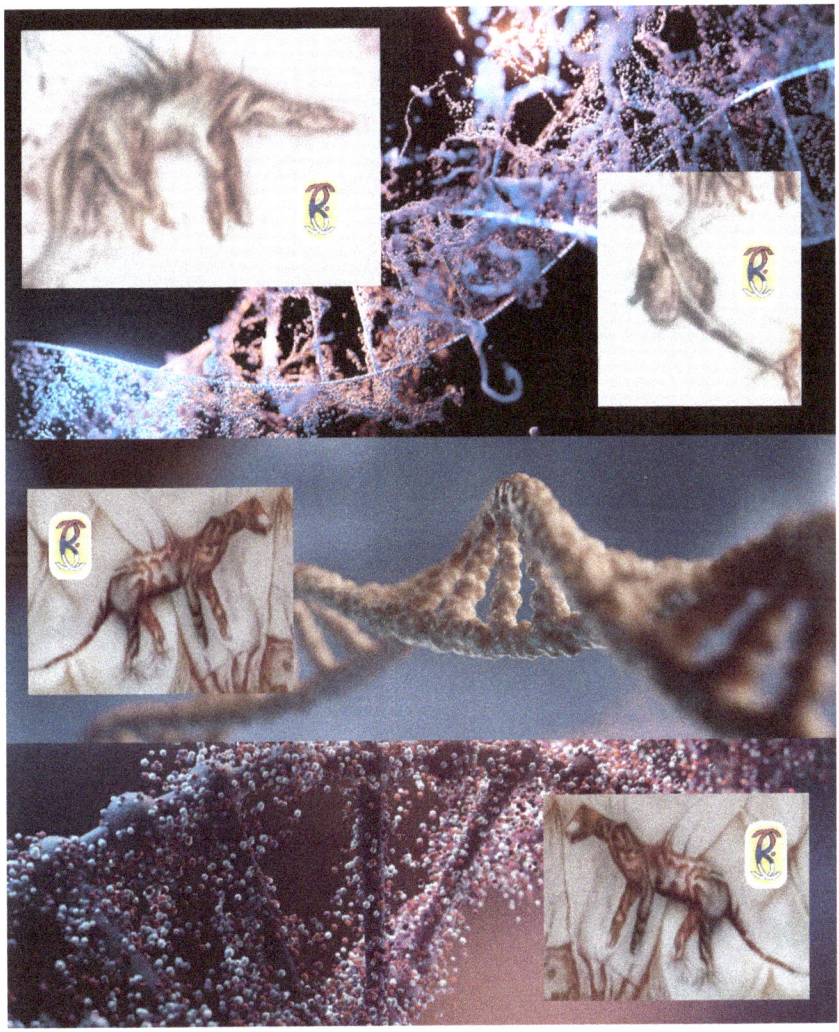

Free to use under Unsplash Licence www.unspash.com

Chapter 19
Undersea Stargates and Bases

(Author's Original Artwork – 1979)

Stargates are also under deep waters. They are what we call: DIMENSIONAL TRIANGLE SHAPES or a POWERFUL MAGNETIC ENERGY DEVICE using VACUUM POWER that can easily interact with objects carrying electronic devices.

As a result, many disappearances have taken place at sea, with some ocean floors looking like grave sites. The vacuum power of these Stargates can be very strong, and can pull ships down from the surface of the ocean.

Under deep waters exist bases and cities created by star entities, some of which are half a million years old. They reside deep within the Mariana Trench, Lake Baikal in Russia, and other places not reachable by humans.

The space entities have unfinished business here on our

planet. Stage by stage, from the beginning, until now, they have taken us through "The Time Sailing Periods", trying to reach certain level as they plan to take us back to that very first stage of our beginning by cutting our Earth population; and then slowly repopulating through pattern stages as they did before.

The Swimmers of Lake Baikal. Found 1982 by Russian Navy Divers.
Unfinished Evolution or New Evolution or The Swimmers of Lake Baikal. Shigir Idol-Baikal Lake Russia approximately 11500 year old.

Chapter 20
Stars Wars Superiority

(Author's Original Artwork – 1979)

Star wars in the past have been between Extra-Terrestrials fighting for new territories called the Milky Way, and other galaxies and planets are also being colonised. Somebody always arrives first, and then those who arrive second attempt to remove them by force, often starting an intergalactic war. Whichever alien race has the superior technology are more often than not the victors.

Inside huge craters are where the previous SPACE EXTRA-TERRESTRIALS expeditions created stations for further activities and commitments. Suddenly, they were attacked by a more advanced Space Civilisation. Their bases were hit by a Super Advanced Weapon, causing what we see now as a massive crater-shape.

It reminds me of "THE AFRICAN EYE" case. It could be the Atlantians of the Atlantis Civilisation. The Atlantis civilisation was between Malta, Libya, Sicily, and Greece.

If Atlantis was above the Mediterranean Sea today, then the Mediterraneans would not have access to sail to Atlantis, because before that "BIG FLOOD" the Gibraltar as we call it today, was naturally closed and was unpassable to sail through.

NASA'S satellite's image of the African Sahara eye was lost in 2005, but rediscovered in 2018 by Scott Tilley.

Free to use under
Unsplash Licence
www.unspash.com

Chapter 21
Fauna and Flora of The First Settlements – Prehistoric Time

(Author's Original Artwork – 1979)

In the picture shown, you can see the first stage of the experiments to stabilise a new environment and create conditions for basic fauna and flora to thrive, setting up for a human existence. This is the pattern routine of HIGH ADVANCED SPACE LABORATORIES used by the same advanced star entities.

SUPER HIGH TECHNOLOGY Spaceships carry the ingredients and the technology to create a high temperature magnetic field beam to transfer floating gold dust into a lake using an advanced technology process.

By injecting gold dust into a lake using an advanced method of smelting gold fragments to create an electrolysis system, with the support of electromagnetic plasma energy, they are able to finalise the process of restoring drinkable water.

The process eliminates all poisons and carcinogenic elements which would otherwise be detrimental to the fauna and flora that rely on a water source.

The "MIXTURE" of the advanced ingredients structure, and the process used to create it, will be a mystery to us for many centuries. It's part of the inability of our fixed IQ Co census as a limited CONTEXT interrupted by NEW DNA.

There is as well a process of forming and experimenting with a lake's water-liquid.

Relating to BLOOD GROUPS – BLOOD CHEMICAL STRUCTURES stored for ESSENTIAL EMERGENCIES.

In other similar cases, newborn planets are used to take samples of already formed lakes with the prefabrications of FUTURE BLOOD GROUPS AND DNA/S!

The animals in the picture CREATED in AN ADVANCED LAB are unknown to us and have never been fully exposed as AN ARCHEOLOGICAL FINDING.

Animals were designed to be adopted into all environmental ADVANTAGES and DISADVANTAGES.

All small and big sites of the past civilisations were engineered from the world experimental laboratories scattered around the world with a similar patten.

49

Chapter 22
Antarctica Civilisations

(Author's Original Artwork – 1979)

In Antarctica, I do believe there is an existing FROZEN CITY and its base is under the mountain shaped like a pyramid-Mountain Peak.

There would be spaceships and launchers as part of the city buildings. To get access to that advanced alien city you need to dig through the thick ice above the FROZEN CITY or go under THE FROZEN SEAWATER section.

It would be difficult to reach because of the extreme barriers, including intense magnetic fields. The other option to reach there would be a global weather changing pattern relating to our climate.

If they allowed us access, since they control that technology. There might also be an ADVANCED TECHNOLOGY GRAVE UNDER THE FROZEN ICE OF ANTARCTICA AND THE ARCTIC.

The magnetic field is in a very high alert, and is being used to hide perfect bases of high advanced intelligent technology for the further continuation of their earth projects, creativities and experiments.

The high intelligent entities using that base are able to come and go using inter-dimensional Stargates.

That whole area is circled with high levels of magnetic fields and constant unknown energy "CODEXLY" protected, which is almost impossible to access.

There is an inheritance of the Atlantians knowledge probably in the same setup of shape and structures. The earth could be artificially rebuilt as the moon from the same entities!

Chapter 23
Olmecs Arrival By Plasma Star Gate

(Author's Original Artwork – 1979)

When extraterrestrials explored North America using advanced roving vehicles and Stargates, they left behind traces of symbiosis between certain plants. This may have been caused by traces of plant spores on their roving vehicle.

The physical samples can be found in some countries around the world. It has been theorised that plant spores and other plant seeds have been spread to different continents in the past.

Magnetic fields are also found in some areas where Stargates were/and still are present. Stargates can be opened using natural magnetic fields or with high advanced technology combined.

Thousands of years ago magnetic spot-fields were difficult to find, but have become more present today because of modern technology.

Stargates were the ADVANCED TECHNOLOGY of THE NON HUMAN UNDERSTANDING WAY OF USAGE. A Magnetic Field device built on an important ADVANCED NETWORK SPOT.

The HANDSETS that have been shown all around the world from the Sumerians, Maya, and Incas, were presenting Remote Reception Tracers and Navigators.

The Handset was A STAR GATE'S KEY CODE – Reception, Tracer and Navigator to reach hidden magnetic field spots all around the Globe. IT WAS AN OPTIONAL DEVICE.

The one who CARRIED that HAND DEVICE was usually a King, Leader or GOD, proclaimed by ADVANCED CIVILISATIONS OF RULING ENTITIES COMMITTEE OF THE EARTH at that time.

They might be back after a certain time, after many Earth Catastrophes, when our planet will need to be repaired and revitalised. They were, and are constant space travelers, observers, and messengers.

Olmecs-Mexico 3500 year ago

Chapter 24
ENDLESS RECIPROCALS

"FROM HUMAN FLESH INTO THE ARTIFICIAL INTELIGENCE TRASH!"

A social and economic society starts with a Primitive, Free Spirits Society. It's based on sharing to survive and keep reproduction going.

After the primitive equal society we got slavery. The freedom of The Free Spirit Primitive Society had been taken away, and those left to survive with others occupied their already established community's hunting grounds, and lakes and rivers for fishing.

As time was passing by, the Super Supreme Elite (S.S. Elite) changed the status of slavery into another form of servitude by way of the social status serfdom. That major change was reflected in agricultural labouring.

As more time passed by, the status of serfdom had been replaced by Manorialism. Free Labour – servants, and a market orientated over peasants and agricultural fields.

Afterwards, the hierarchical system called Feudalism was introduced, with land ownership based on the power of Lords, who protected serfs in exchange for labour.

After Feudalism, Capitalism took over, which is based on private ownership of productions relating to land, factories, and free markets.

When Capitalism collapsed, Socialism took over, promoting social equality, social ownership, and social welfare.

Communism was a continuation of Socialism, passing all ownerships and rights to labour and society.

Afterwards, variations of Socialism-Communism, Socialism-Capitalism, and Communism-Capitalism were introduced.

A New Era of Social and Economical Systems are on the horizon.

1-AI -Artificial Intelligence.

2-AGI-Artificial General Intelligence.

3-AAI-Artificial Advanced Intelligence.

4-ASI-Artifical Super Intelligence.

5-ASSI -Artificial Super Supreme Intelligence.

6-ASSGI-Artificial Super Supreme General Intelligence.

7-ASSAI-Artificial Super Supreme Advanced Intelligence.

8-ASMI-Artificial Super Matrix Intelligence.

9-ASGMI-Artificial Super Matrix General Intelligence.

10-ASAMI-Artificial Super Advanced Matrix Intelligence.

11-ASSMI -Artificial Super Supreme Matrix Intelligence.

<u>INTERSTELAR COSMIC KNOWLEGE</u>

12-ASCI-Artificial Super Cosmic Intelligence.

13-ASGCI-Artificial Super General Cosmic Intelligence.

14-ASACI-Artificial Super Advanced Cosmic Intelligence.

15-ASSCI-Artificial Super Supreme Cosmic Intelligence

They can be converted into individual time dimensions for certain usages and purposes. "JUST LIKE A HUMAN DREAM CAN BE TIMELY CONVERTED INTO THE PAST, PRESENT, AND FUTURE!"

Everything will pass by, but The Original Time will remain endlessly here and out there. We are always comparing time with evolution, civilisations, history, weather, demography, geography, etc. But we never compare the previous with The Original Time, because The Original Time is like a Fixed Observer that never Changes. The Time Helpers past, present, and future, are partly belonging to The Original Time.

When the human population slides down to 5% - they will be distinguished as ex-majorities. Then Human Civilisation will fulfil that endless-Reciprocal stage of evolution.

5% of human civilisation will remain in underground bases, unless they convert mining craters into new bases with a special glass dome to be 100% protected.

Taking part in orders from CREATORS, the S.S. Elite will start everything all over again, just like before, with a Primitive Free Spirit Society.

Everything was thoughtfully planned much before humans began to walk the Earth. Designed, cloned, and taken again from their well established Artificial Super Supreme Advanced Matrix Laboratories, perhaps half a million years ago or longer. The project I would name:"FROM A FLASH TO TRASH, AND ALL OVER AGAIN! " (Endless -Reciprocals.)

Those Millions of years of Reversible Projects Came from surrounded Galaxies - Milky-ways, and Parallel Universes. Brought by ASSAMASSCAI -Artificial Super Supreme Matrix and Super Supreme Cosmic Advanced Intelligence. It happened just like a flash from a camera-travelling to us by the speed of the Cosmic Lights, Possibly from Dying Stars, Parallel Universes that surround our

Solar System, or Cosmic Travelling Dimensions, looking for a place to settle permanently. It could also be from black holes nearby, as a product of their outlets relating to mixed energy, or as a final filterised product of the pure new energy, which was left over from a black hole's exit storage of a previous unextinguished or non-distinct energy. Black Hole projects are futuristic"Cosmic Seeds", relating to the beginning of the environment to satisfy all human existence.

If we look at the experimental pressures on humans with all kinds of abuses, suffering, mental torture, and IQ manipulations, they will always be there in a different way periodically, as a social and economical excuse. Not only humans suffer under those experiments in circling projects. Flora, Fauna, and the Environment suffer under the same unpleasant treatment.

That's why Mother Earth - Nature fights responsibly to save us. How long that fight will take place is up to our understanding of how important it is to us not to be distinguished and believe in supporting Mother Earth - and her Natural Resistance Abilities.

"Between the lies, this will never look like The Natural Evolution of Human principals, but more closely look like the Human Misery of Artificial Existence!"

"Every micro-programme hidden from our naked eye in our system is a Permanent Parameter of DNA Inheritance.

For example: "A Human gamete contains memory of a DNA Microchip Programme created through A Super Supreme Advanced Season. That's why the birthday of a human being is not accidental."

FORESEE AGENDA

IN THE YEAR 2035:
AI-ARTIFICIAL INTELLIGENCE REACHES 35% GLOBALLY.

IN THE YEAR 2070:
AGI -ARTIFICAL GENERAL INTELIGENCE REACHES 55% GLOBALLY.

IN THE YEAR 2105:
AAI-ARTIFICIAL ADVANCED INTELIGENCE REACHES 65% GLOBALLY.

IN THE YEAR 2160:
ASI-ARTIFICAL SUPER INTELIGENCE REACHES 75% GLOBALLY.

IN THE YEAR 2195:
ASSI-ARTIFICIAL SUPER SUPREME INTELIGENCE REACHES 85% GLOBALLY.

IN THE YEAR 2230:
ASSMI-SUPER SUPREME MATRIX INTELIGENCE
REACHES 95% GLOBALLY

"5% OF THE ORIGINAL HUMAN
WILL GLOBALLY REMAIN TO BE ABLE TO START THAT ENDLESS
PROGRAMME OF RECIPROCALS!"
PREHISTORIC MAN UNTIL MODERN MAN:

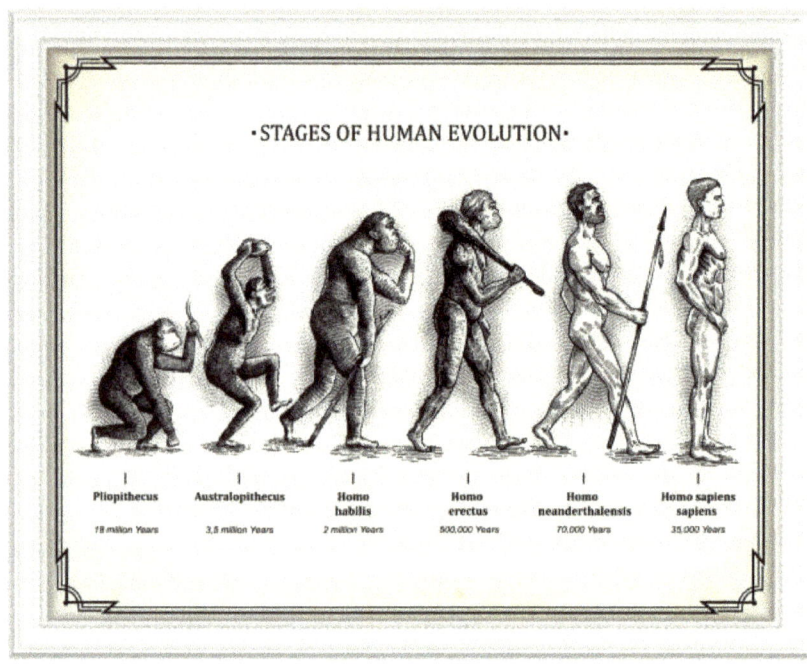

The next two stages of human evolution will be to wipe out all memory of humanity in the following stages:

Reciprocals Waste

Reciprocals Recycle

The Proofs Of My Original Pictures

Magazine Galaxy
Published 1982

Artists Of
New Visions

**Chapter 5
Sleeping City
Twin Towers
NY USA**

The original date of the original artwork with artist's original signature.

Comparison of Civilisations, Humanoid Species and Entities

LEPENSKI VIR

Lepenski Vir – Around 11,500 years ago and today the same location.

LEPENSKI VIR PIT

SATURNIA-ITALY: Around 11,500 years ago, the area of what today we know as Rome, Italy, was inhabited by small, scattered tribes and settlements, likely hunter-gatherers. There are no specific records or archaeological sites of that particular period. The first archaeological evidence starts to emerge between 1000 BC and 800 BC with Iron Age huts, pottery, shrines, defensive walls and burial grounds.

HELLENIC-GREECE: Around 11,500 years ago, there were no recognised human structures, because the people were nomadic hunter-gatherers, preferring to move from place to place with the seasons.

Archaeological evidence of the Neolithic Period showed that human presence existed around the Acropolis area before 3000 BC. There was evidence of stone tools and shallow wells.

Athens' recorded history spans over 3400 years, but there is evidence that humans were in that location much earlier.

Vinča Civilisation

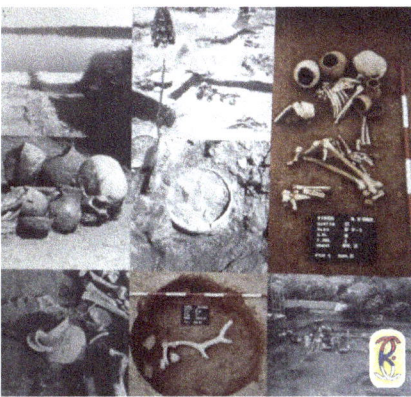

The Vinca Civilisation is around 7500 years old, dating back to 5400 BC – 4600 BC. They were based in south Europe, which today is modern Serbia. It was an early part of The Neolithic Period of history. The Vinca were the first metal working society in Europe. They worked with copper, casting tools and decorative objects. They created things like chisels, hammers, axes, needles and beads. Their first writing of symbols predates Mesopotamia.

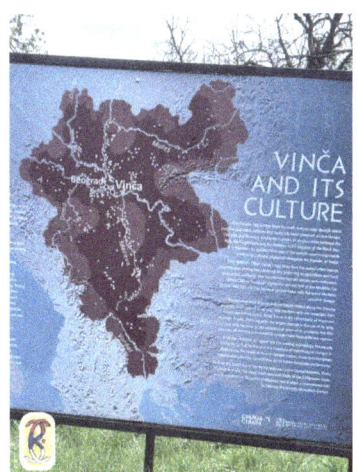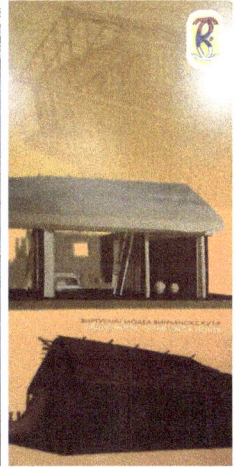

Lady of Vinca approx. 7500 years ago

The Vinca people introduced the first farming and cultivation of crops, like wheat, barley, and flax. They used cows to plough the soil; they also introduced oats as well. The Vinca people also created distinctive clay figures. They had no defensive walls around their society and were a peaceful people. They introduced the first forms of urban development.

THE VINČA CIVILISATION HAD A WIDE INFLUENCE ON OTHER NEOLITHIC GROUPS IN EUROPE, ESPECIALLY IN METALLURGY, AGRICULTURE, AND WRITING SYMBOLS!"

SATURNIA-ITALY 7500 YEARS AGO: The Vinca civilisation predated the Saturnia civilisation in metallurgy, agriculture, writing symbols, and urban development.

HELLENIC-GREECE: 7500 YEARS AGO: The Vinca Civilisation predated the Hellenic civilisation in metallurgy, agriculture, writing symbols, and urban development.

MESOPOTAMIA-IRAQ: 7500 YEARS AGO The Vinca Civilisation predated the Mesopotamian civilisation in metallurgy, agriculture, writing symbols, and urban development.

KEMET-EGYPT 7500 YEARS AGO: The Vinca Civilisation predated the Kemet civilisation in metallurgy, agriculture, writing symbols, and urban development.

Comparison of Past Entities

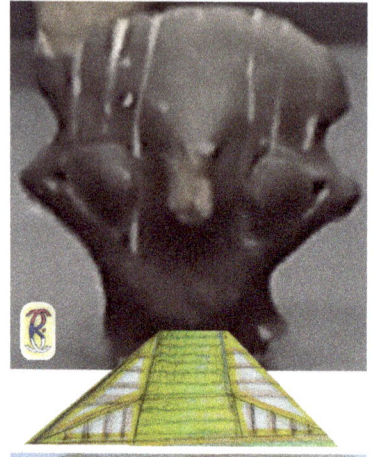

Vinča Civilisation Head of unknown inhabitant approximately 7500 years old. Vinča Neolithic Culture.

The Head of Narmer First King of Predinasty Egypt. Ruled Egypt 5100 years ago.

The Head of King Khufu or Pharoe. Ruled Egypt 4500 years ago.

Comparison of Vinča's Artifact

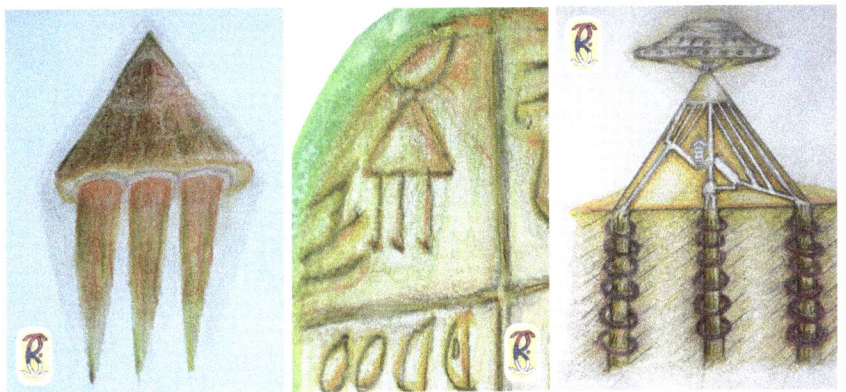

Vinča's artifact shows possible 7500 year ago flying object or 4500 years ago Cheops Great Pyramid with a flying object above it.

Comparison of Entities

Thoth Egypt around 8000 years ago.
Thoth of Vinča around 7500 years ago.

Comparison of Entities

Approximatively 7500 year old mystery figure found in Vinca Neolithic culture today Serbia.

Approximatively 7000 year old mystery figure found in Ubaid Mesopotamia today Iraq.

Comparison Of Flying Objects

Vinča-Serbia flying object 7500 years old.

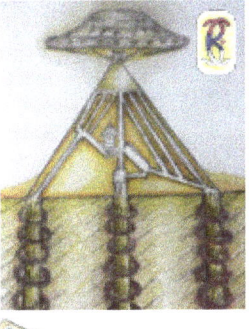

Khufu Dinasty-Egypt 4500 years ago.

Olmecs-Mexico flying object 3500 years ago.

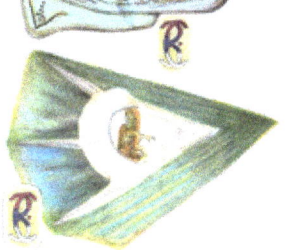

Visoki Dečani Fresco Serbian Orthodox Church 700 year ago.

"All of them were periodicaly used for their scattered missions around the earth continents from their nearby bases conducted by cosmic codes from the mighty one!"

Comparison of Entities

Shigir Idol figure from Baikal Lake Russia Approximatively 11,500 years old.

Vinča Idol figure approximately 7500 years old Neolithic time Serbia.

MY THOUGHTS ON MIXED TOPICS

The Sumerian tablets remind me of an ELECTRONIC MICROCHIP with FRAMED SECTIONS of WRITING that came from COMPUTERISED PROGRAM SIGN FORMS, using a ROBOTIC SYSTEM.

The Sumerians, Assyrians, and Mesopotamians had tablets similar to the ones today with SCREEN PICTURES which is a continuation of the PROGRAMS SIGN FORMS.

They have been upgraded today for the general public for their ease of visual understanding. Like today's BILLBOARDS – the ancients had Computerised Programs Sign Forms, including fashion designed engravings of the handsets, jewelery, clothes, hats, and shoes, like we see today in
shop windows. IT'S CIRCLE OF REPEATING.

WE ARE TRYING TO UNDERSTAND THE STRANGE FACTS PASSED TO US TO LOOK AT AND WORK OUT FROM A HUMAN PERSPECTIVE.

After all, guessing and finding a half-truth is the only thing left to do, except wait for the Extraterrestrials to explain everything to us to complete our research mission.

TV, phones, computers, media, etc, are used to escape from reality, pulling Earth citizens into it ...to get away from real life, Mother Nature, and God.

The Sumerians were using clay-reeds and wood sticks to write on... but what about advanced laptops or billboards placed inside?

Nibirians Spacecraft?

If you came from space millions of miles away with super advanced technology, even for the 21st century, how they could suddenly drop into a Stone Age time, writing on a clay tablet, ignoring their millions of years of advanced technology. ABSOLUTELY STRANGE!

In a Matrix there is no oxygen... no smell, no sounds and no touch... IT'S A HIGH LEVEL HYPNOTIC STATE OF THE HUMAN IMAGINATION.

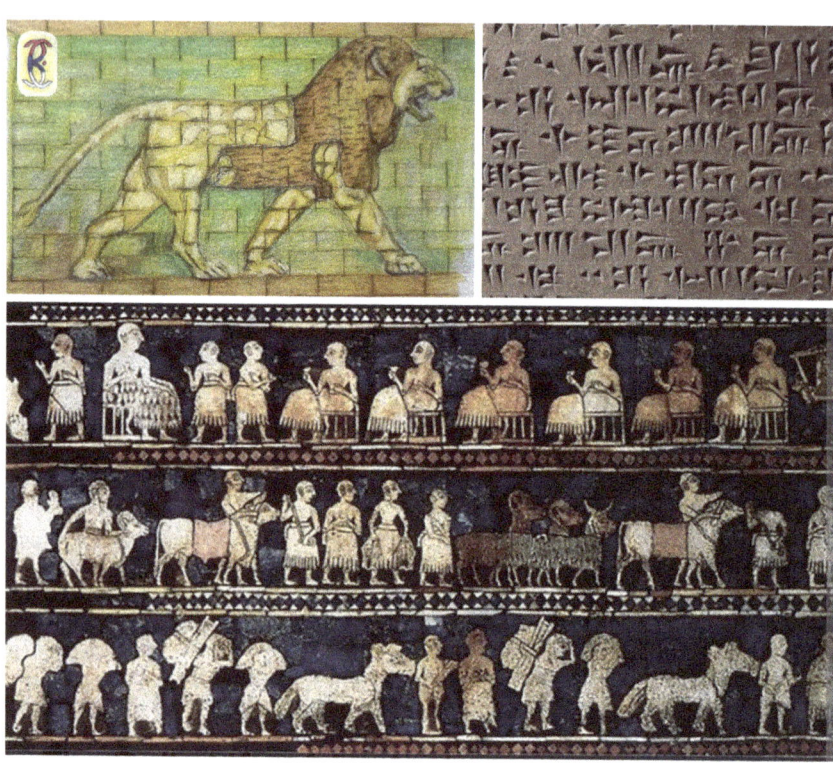

Shutterstock The Sumerians royalty-free images.

We live in a graphic of micro structured world holding us connected with unseen and seen types of textures. Surfacelly as a Mega Texture or Physical Camouflage and under neath it deeper is an unseen Micro Texture holding our emotions of our spiritual behavings.

"What we drew and engraved out side of us that's what we are inside of us!"

That kind of BRAINWASH is a KEY lock to get you into THEIR MATRIX. It comes from experimental computerised projects to break human natural and spiritual barriers as an easy way to be sucked into the IMAGINARY ARTIFICIAL COMPLEX...

To escape the Matrix, most of the time you have to associate with Mother Nature, avoiding all types of intense mainstream or other media.

The Matrix is an artificial computerised project meant to be informational. It is designed for humans to accept it as a visual imaginary bridge to take them to the next imaginary level.

When you purposefully crucified the Son of God to spare Satan, it was the momentum of the Devil's Era of belief. We will always sorrow, praise, comfort, respect, and believe in Jesus, but we never blame Satan. We never talk bad things about Satan. We never say MONEY IS THE DEVIL'S WEAPON... WITH ALL IMMORAL, NON-HUMAN, AND GREED OF NEEDS.

The spirit is a human resource of navigating feelings and surviving. People's longevity of life in the past must be related to the speed of time, such as 1 day equaling 10 days.

We might someday experience the Holographic Universe and activities, even if we aren't ready for it with our senses, as they do not belong to that. The Holographic Universe does not own human senses....It's an individual purpose of usage.

There are perhaps no wormholes in the Milky Way, but instead placed inside an ex-black matter fabric. If we use a Web Telescope to look into the Nibirum Solar System and the planet Nibiru there is not much proof of those past traveling activities 500,000 years ago, except if they have underground bases.

If the universe is empty for that reason I do presume that the extraterrestrials live in an unknown, advanced level of dimensions upgraded from millions of years ago. They say there are 11 dimensions. What about SUB-DIMENSIONS and SUPRIME DIMENSIONS? All races are artificial mutations of the same base of DNA...

BLACK HOLES may not be what we think, but space REGULATORS of REDUCING nearby planets and making space for NEW ONES from A NEW ENERGY coming out as A SHAPE OF WHITE LIGHT.

A spaceship owner hunting with bows & arrows, and spears seems implausible, but those weapons would have been more advanced than the primitive versions used by early man. After all, who taught man how to make such weapons in the first place? Darkness with no light. Cold with no heating system. Did they feel that?... always mentioning Gold, Gemstones, etc. Robots are impervious to variations in temperature to a certain extent but humans are not. These stories seem to have been created on purpose to catch somebody's attention and make others believe it... too many nonsense ideas and lies.

Traveling in a spaceship from Naruk to Uru in less than 10 seconds. The Sumerians calculated years were 1 year =50 years? If dogs and cats lives are measured 1 human year to 7 years for dogs and cats, then it makes sense for star extraterrestrials to have a different lifespan.

The span of time is not up to us to fix. It's part of A COSMIC ENERGY, which is why time is not real or as important to people as money. COSMIC ENERGY has downloaded time and lifespan from space, GIFTING humans with that – GOD WISH.

I wonder why Toth did not pass those numbers from Emerald tablets to the Egyptians. We can see it on a tablet repeating numerals 1 2 3 4 7 9? They are 31000 years before the Egyptians written numerals 5000 years ago. These numbers are 36,000 old, and the Egyptian Numeral system is not even close to those exposed numbers on the Emerald Tablet.

The question is, how can the advanced Numeral System presented 36,000 years ago, the same one being used today, not be the same as the one used 5000 years ago? The figure – Toth – was ruling, building, and educating those civilisations?

Something is not right if they were using numbers as letters. If that's the case, it looks like a green computer screen. Somebody was copying from it into emerald tablets and not paying attention. They were mixing codes of numerals with letters. They left it like that for over 34000 years. Why have the numerals been changed? Maybe somebody copied that again and used them as today's numerals?

The tablet is a perfect, advanced and smooth piece of work. It looks like somebody used high advanced technology to create it. It could have been a Milling Stone Program of tools. The letters/numeral shapes are perfectly lined up. The spaces in-between are smooth and definitive. Chisel tools did not exist at that time, yet the perfectly smooth tablet looks younger and newer.

It is comparable with an example from the Vinca Civilisation in Serbia approximately 7500 years old. It looks like they were hanging around each other in the same period of time, or they may have been connected by water or land roads.

The pyramids were built on a NATURAL HILL that previously existed. They were built by Ancient African People, similar to the DOGON tribe. They lived, as they do today, in West Africa. The other tribes lived in North Africa, and were named the Nubians. In the past, they have been used to build the Gaza Pyramids because of their good Masonry skills. The knowledge they learned came from extraterrestrial visitors. They have been constantly observed by Star

Men.

The Dogon people gained vast Astrological Knowledge from alien visitation, and they kept it secret until these very last days. The other African tribes involved in the Giza Project could be the Badari and Naquada peoples.

The strange, space ENTITIES appearances were helping them to lift and shape heavy blocks.

They only came in and out from their only known dimension to satisfy building needs. The dimensions are timeless and short space cuts. 500,000 Years for us, but for them it might only be five seconds using super advanced technology.

In general, the energy is the source of knowledge and miracles!

Energy is a silent, invisible connector for our existence. The cosmic energy holds those three

Miracle code numbers 3, 6, & 9, connecting us and "the others" with the various existing energy sources traveling around, and inside of us. They might preset the code called "flower of life".

If they say time doesn't exist, then how can it be corrected? Example: if we are counting this time as the 21st Century, what about the space entities traveling from 5000th Century and visiting us in those unaccounted times, plus 21 Centuries back? We are talking about the UNIVERSE'S COMPUTERISED SYSTEM ACCELERATED BY COSMIC ENERGY

AS AN IMPORTANT FACTOR. Passing through certain places in the universe after certain times, and at the right time, must be easy for ESTIMATES, as we are using it and living with those same numeral system programs today.

The birth of the universe acts as an EXPLOSION. The death of the universe acts as a BLACK HOLE. The universe is both creative and destructive at the same time.

The same spot in a universe with two different PERFORMING FORMS is in a constant state of repeating.

"JESUS KNEW THE CODES FOR STAR GATES AND THE CODE OF THE HIGHEST DIMENSION THAT HE COULD'VE REACHED THE GOD – HIS FATHER – AT ANY TIME.

That's why he was so dangerous in the prospect of "RULING ON THE EARTH!"

Jesus' bloodline came from the GARDEN OF EDEN, a privileged place where special ones are chosen by God/s.

If Jesus was a God, he could've easily saved himself from crucifixion. But because he was very important and loyal to God, God resurrected him. Jesus is the only one who knew the code of how to properly be connected to God.

People wonder why some Christians pray with a little candle. If the Devil tries to talk to them during the praying session, the candle blaze will burn his tongue!

If we could rid the world of all kinds of antennas surrounding us, we would have a better RECEPTION WITH GOD. GOD-MESSENGER – PEOPLE PRESENT WITH THE DIVINE TRIANGLE OF THE FLOWER OF LIFE.

Jesus' bloodline background could be related to his ancestors from the Garden of Eden. The Turin shroud of Jesus was a three dimensional Leonardo Da Vinci GEOMETRICAL CODE EXPERIMENT, which was typical for his ADVANCED EXPERIMENTS and CREATIVITIES, using a European man as a model.

It is Comparable with a well known Da Vinci PROPORTIONAL MALE/FEMALE CODE.

It could be the first of Leonardo's experiment with A NEGATIVE PHOTOGRAPHY EXPOSURE.

The Egyptian pyramids represent the DIVINE TRIANGLE OF THE FLOWER OF LIFE.

Gobekli Tepe was a Research Lab relating to the creation of a new species, and saving an already existing one.

They are 19th the same letters or symbols of the 27th all up of each Vinci's and Etruscan's .

IF WE LOOK AT THE OLDEST ETRUSCAN MAPS THERE ARE LOT OF NAMES RELATING TO THE VINČA REGION OF THE AREA

CERE VOLCI KLUZI KUMA RUMA-ROME VAJA

DRECIJ – THOSE NAMES ARE FROM VINČA REGION AREA FROM AROUND 7500 AND TODAY SERBIA AND INCLUDING A PART BALKAN

It means Etruscans lived near the Vinča or they were visiting Vinča from West side of Europe or from South Europe or from EuroAsia 3000 years ago and staying in Vinča Region minimum for 200 years where they gain the most of the knowledge and taken with them to ETRURIA – Today Italy Vinci or Vinča has the same meaning Settlement.

I do believe Leonardo da Vinci's ancestors were Etruscans not only by his family name, but by his a great knowledge about almost everything. And it was not hard for the smartest man in a world to find out about his back ground.

Meanings Of Those Names:
Volci – Where they raised keep oxen
Kluzi – Appendix
Ruma – Rome
Vaja – She is strong and inbreakable Kuma –
The best girlfriend
Cere – Where grows CERRIS Tree
Kosa – Meadow in an Angle, Human Hair or Sickle.

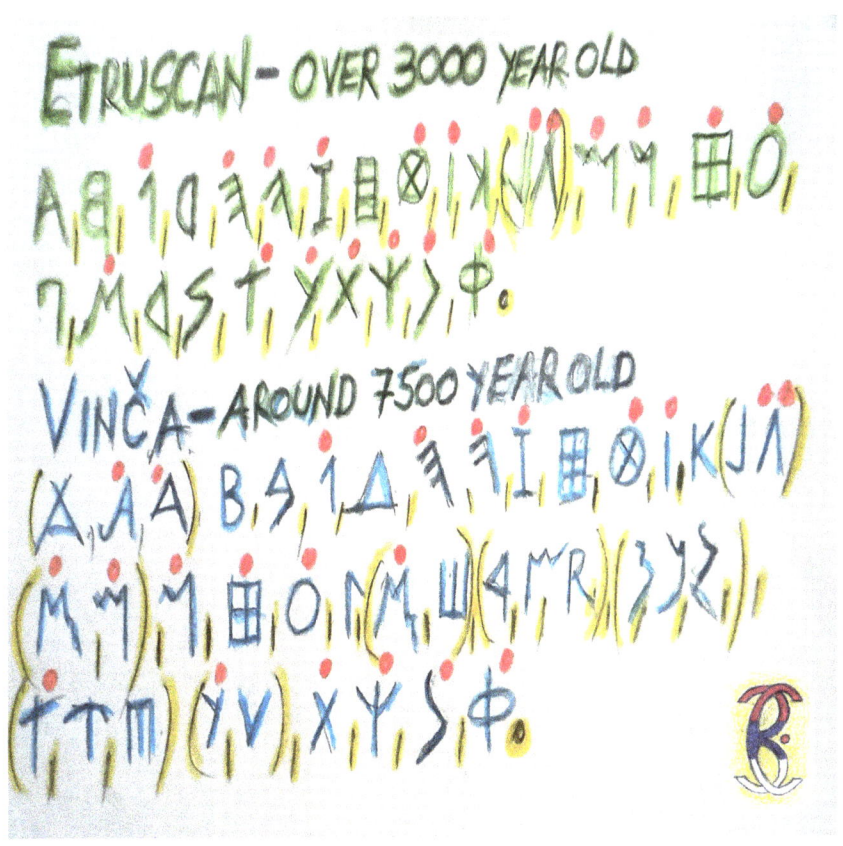

Free to use under the Unsplash License www.unsplash.com

A statue of Leonardo Da Vinci in Rome, Italy

Jesus Turin Shroud in Vatican Rome, Italy

Praying is an advanced level of the spiritual dedication to be connected to the Lord Jesus, the Son and Messenger of the almighty God. Jesus' spoke and used the Aramaic language to preach and communicate with people. Most Christian priests cannot speak Aramaic, which is a disadvantage to cope with peoples prayers, due to the meanings of other language translations. It should be passed through a priest that is knowledgeable in the Aramaic tongue. This missing link is why many important wishes could not be finalised through prayer.

IMPORTANT MESSAGE

(Author's Original Artwork – 1979)

We should Love everybody around the Globe, Being Alive, Happy, and Content.

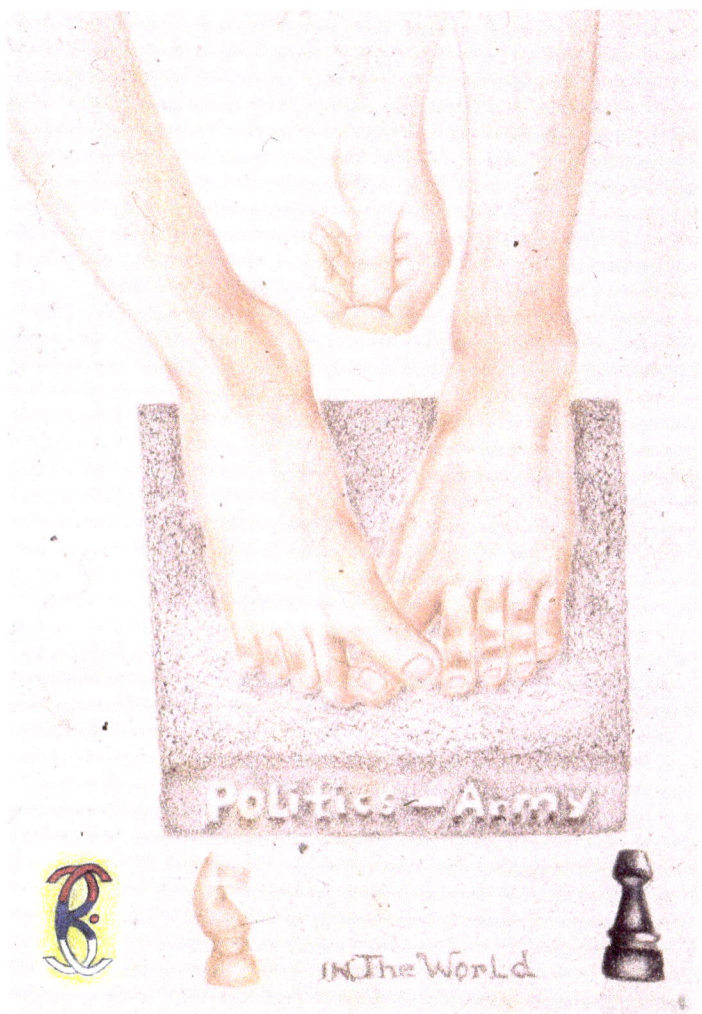

Instead we are making Wars, Killings, Miseries, Sicknesses, and Poverties.

www.ingramcontent.com/pod-product-compliance
Lightning Source LLC
Chambersburg PA
CBHW042118100526

44587CB00025B/4114